SPRINTING FROM TH

SPRINTING FROM THE GRAVEYARD

Goran Simić

English versions by David Harsent

Sam —

Much Love

Oxford   Toronto   New York

OXFORD UNIVERSITY PRESS

Publication Day

20/3/97

1997

Oxford University Press, Great Clarendon Street, Oxford OX2 6DP
Oxford New York
Athens Auckland Bangkok Bogota Bombay Buenos Aires
Calcutta Cape Town Dar es Salaam Delhi Florence Hong Kong
Istanbul Karachi Kuala Lumpur Madras Madrid Melbourne
Mexico City Nairobi Paris Singapore Taipei Tokyo Toronto
and associated companies in
Berlin Ibadan

Oxford is a trade mark of Oxford University Press

English versions © David Harsent 1997
from original poems in Bosnian by Goran Simić

First published in Oxford Poets
as an Oxford University Press paperback 1997

British Library Cataloguing in Publication Data
Data available

Library of Congress Cataloging in Publication Data
Simić, Goran, 1952–
[Poems. English. Selections]
Sprinting from the graveyard / Goran Simić ; English versions by
David Harsent.
p. cm. -- (Oxford poets)
1. Sarajevo (Bosnia and Hercegovina)--History--Siege, 1992–1996–Poetry.
2. Simić, Goran, 1952– --Translations into English.
I. Harsent, David. II. Title. III. Series.
PG1419.29.I36A25 1997   891.8'215--dc20   96-44122
ISBN 0-19-288023-3

1 3 5 7 9 10 8 6 4 2

Typset by Rowland Phototypesetting Limited
Printed in Hong Kong

For Amela, Luna and Darije
who lived this book in Sarajevo

FOREWORD

TOGETHER WITH his wife, Amela, and their two young children, Goran Simić saw out the siege of Sarajevo. Most of the poems in this collection were written under siege. It's difficult to expand much on this information without wanting to enter a political debate. One might, for example, note that Simić is a Serb, his wife a Muslim; but it would be crucial to add that handy obfuscations that traded off so-called 'ethnicity' were routinely used by politicians in Western countries to present the Bosnian conflict as, simply, a civil war that had been going on and off the boil for centuries. Should we try to make sense of it? Should we look for a political narrative? Invasion; butchery; rape as a weapon of war; the inspired use of the word 'cleansing' to suggest the riddance of *filth, scum, vileness, pollution, garbage, disease*; news pictures of concentration camps like old photos come suddenly into focus ... The message, the 'official attitude', seemed to be that while it was okay to care—no, it was *essential* to care—there was little we could do. It was a mess, but it was *their* mess, and that was a comforting thought.

Blame is a pretty big issue in all wars. The conflict in Bosnia seemed to need it more than most. Everyone wanted to know who was to blame. Who was *most* to blame. Who was to blame on this occasion; who was to blame on that. If you didn't think too carefully about it, everyone could seem to blame; that was a happy notion. Or else, even more useful, history might be blamed — as if, ultimately, blame itself were to blame.

Goran Simić's poems don't apportion any dole of blame though, as a man living with his family in the old quarter of the city throughout the three-year terror, it's safe to assume that he formed an opinion. His poems, however, refuse to be polemical; his purpose, it's clear, is to record:

> I wanted to write poems like newspaper reports,
> so heartless, so cold,
> that I could forget them, forget them
> in the same moment that someone might ask me,
> 'Why do you write poems like newspaper reports?'

The note of irony, here and elsewhere, is one of the things that make Simić's poems so compelling: at times the unadorned record, at others the wry metaphor, or the bleak laughter of the eyewitness. It says: blame doesn't come into it; what's happening is too terrible for blame to make a difference. It says: We know who's to blame and we could name names. In fact, we will, we will. But in the meantime, look at this: this is what's happening; this is how it is.

In making these English versions I have been greatly indebted to Amela Simić, who supplied me with word-for-word translations of her husband's poems—literal texts that made no concession to interpretation. I used these as cribs to get what I wanted.

My purpose was to make new poems in English from this raw material. All I had to go on—all I asked to have—were the poems' bare bones. I made changes, some extravagant; excisions, some radical; and additions, some substantial. The idea (it might be guessed) was to preserve the spirit of the poems by breaking the chains of literalism. In fact, the *idea* was to make composition something more fundamental, involving and risky than a system of equivalence that allowed itself a few minor textual liberties— the choice of an English idiom, say, or a shuffling of stanzas.

There's nothing particularly new about this technique, though I think I may have taken it further than most.

DAVID HARSENT

GORAN SIMIĆ was born in Bosnia in 1952. His poetry, essays and reviews have appeared in all the leading journals of the former Yugoslavia. His plays for children were widely staged by Bosnian puppet theatres. Before the war, he edited a number of literary magazines, including *Lica*, one of the foremost cultural magazines of its day. He was a founder member of the Bosnia-Herzegovina branch of PEN.

The poems he wrote during the siege of Sarajevo have been published in Bosnia, Slovenia and Serbia (!), as well as appearing in translation in the UK, Finland, Denmark, Norway, Sweden and Germany. He wrote the libretto for the operetta *Europe* to music by Nigel Osborne. The piece was performed in Sarajevo in February 1995. His play for children, *A Sarajevan Fairy Tale*, was produced by the Young People's Theatre in Sarajevo and later toured Germany and Switzerland.

In 1995 he received a 'Freedom to Write' award from the PEN Center, USA west. He and his family now live in Canada.

ACKNOWLEDGEMENTS

Poems from this collection, sometimes in different versions, have previously appeared in *Agenda, Descant* (Toronto), *Casablanca, Poetry Review*, and the *Times Literary Supplement*. Several were heard on Radio 4 in a broadcast from Salisbury Cathedral where they were read as part of the 1995 Remembrance Day service; others were read as part of a Sarajevo feature in *The Usual Suspects* (Radio Scotland), producer Mike Lloyd.

Three of the poems were set as part of the libretto for Nigel Osborne's opera *Sarajevo*, which had its première at the Queen Elizabeth Hall, South Bank, London, in 1994, and were published in the programme for that event.

Together with extracts from letters by Amela Simić, a number of them formed a Radio 3 broadcast called *The Sorrow of Sarajevo*, readers: Julia Watson and Alan Rickman, producer Fiona McLean.

Eight poems appeared as *The Sorrow of Sarajevo*, a limited edition published by Cargo Press (Tregarne, Cornwall).

CONTENTS

DOGS AND BONES

After a few days of war
the Sarajevo streets were a catwalk for dogs:
perfumed dogs, well-groomed dogs, dogs
with cut-glass collars
and not a flea between them. Their owners
had left them as they left
the burning city.

The trash-heaps became
a battlefield where the lapdogs lost
to an army of strays, lean-limbed
and mangy with hate.
Cowering and cleansed, the back-alley refugees
retreated to the doorways
of locked apartments, barking an answer
to each unearthly whistle
as the morning shells came in.

*

. . . one of those locked apartments
where we kicked down the door, searching
for a bastard sniper and found
the skeleton of an old woman, fused
to a kitchen chair, yes, merged with the wood.
She had starved to death
sitting next to a pantry crammed with cans of food.

We spent a long time debating the crucial issue
of her religion. Yackety-yack. We could get no clue
from the photos that littered the place,
or the needlepoint of a knight
and castle, or the hundred
bottles of perfume placed around her bed.
Her piously folded hands remained a secret.

1

It was dawn before the argument died out
and we carried her into the street where dogs
were fighting amid the garbage—
nothing they wouldn't risk,
nothing they wouldn't eat. Who cares,
anyway? Who knows
whether she even believed in God? 'By God,
God will find his hands full
after this war,' someone said, and we fell
silent, pretending not to see
her silly grin, and the sudden silver glint
of the can-opener on its chain
around her neck.

DECORATIONS

When he came back from the war, my grandfather
locked himself up
in the attic and stayed there
two weeks or more. He kept the days
in silence but at night
his moans were so terrible they snuffed
the candles burning beneath
the icon. 'The day he came down,'
my grandmother told us, 'I looked
death in the face.'

When he came back from the war, my father
shrugged off his blood-
stained greatcoat and spilled
a heap of medals from his bag
and went to the attic
without a second glance. Each day,
my mother and I would match
his medals with grandad's, ribbon
for ribbon, star for star; each night we hugged
our pillows not to hear his moans, not to hear
the way he called on his dead friends;
each morning, we placed
their decorations on the windowsill
for passers-by to admire, forgetting
that no one passed our house any more.
'There's a ghost in his overcoat,' my mother said,
'I looked into its eyes.'

This was years ago, but even now
the medals hang there
on the sill. From time to time,
some bureaucrat takes them away,
only to bring them back
after a day or so. Listen,
I wouldn't miss them. I only notice them, now,
when I hear news of the war. All that's really left
of my father, of my grandfather,
is the noise the wind makes when it's cut
by the beams in the attic.

THE SORROW OF SARAJEVO

The Sarajevo wind
leafs through newspapers
that are glued by blood to the street;
I pass with a loaf of bread under my arm.

The river carries the corpse of a woman.
As I run across the bridge
with my canisters of water,
I notice her wristwatch, still in place.

Someone lobs a child's shoe
into the furnace. Family photographs spill
from the back of a garbage truck;
they carry inscriptions:
Love from ... love from ... love ...

There's no way of describing these things,
not really. Each night I wake
and stand by the window to watch my neighbour
who stands by the window to watch the dark.

THE APPRENTICE

Half a lifetime I've been looking
for a language so perfect
that everything will come good
in the moment when my pen meets the paper.

Shadows taught me a little, a little I got
from monuments; sometimes, in the search
for beauty, this *beautiful* language, I kept
the company of ghosts.

These days, I spend more time at funerals
than I spend at my desk ... A book of fairy tales
burns blue-green in the frozen stove
as I warm lime-tea for my sick child.

He sips the tea. The sudden colour
in his cheeks is beautiful,
the colour of health;
and the lime-flower is more beautiful than the rose.

IMAGINATION LOST

Listen, God,
my imagination is wearing out—
can you hear?—my anger
is getting thin, like something
lapped in acid.
All the old mistakes
come round again.
The same wind
on the summer beaches
printing the sand
with the initials of the north.

Listen, God,
this is me, this is someone
coming out of nowhere yet again.
I remember that summer
only by the sun-blots
on my skin. My God,
there is a silence growing here
that my voice likes.
Have you noticed
how much I resemble
my reflection? Have you
noticed that even though
I can still walk through walls
they leave me bruised?
That when I reach up, I get mud
under my fingernails?
Have you noticed
I've run out of questions?

My imagination is wearing out.
Let's say I'm under the sea.
Let's say you've given me fish-eyes.
Let's say you promised
I'd find something down here
on the sea-bed, something
I badly need. Let's say
I don't know what it is.

I don't know what it is,
any more than I understand
your Grand Purpose,
capital-G, capital-P.
I stand in the queue
for answers, where I've stood
a thousand times. You give me
an old man's walking stick,
cut down by an inch or two,
and look me in the eye
and ask yourself: *How come
I have answers to questions
he hasn't thought of yet?*

Here's how I see you,
God: with a chainsaw
over your shoulder,
and you're walking through
a forest, and if you think
of me at all it's only
to despise me, and my imagination
is wearing out, wearing
thin, like that—
look—look there—like that
hoarfrost melting back
into the tree, the very
tree you mean to fell.

VICTORY

I was passing through a country,
some foreign country,
when I realised they'd won
the World Cup that same day.
That very day! Imagine it—everyone
was on the street with national flags,
with hunting horns, with 'Victory!
Victory!' Such patriots!
A rich sight in a rich country.
After they'd gone—flags and horns
and 'Victory'—I noticed
someone had stolen my bag of food.

*

There's a photograph of my father
carrying a sub-machine gun,
a Russian gun (only the best
for the best) and walking
into our town from the hills.
He's yelling, 'Victory! Victory!'—
thin as death and wearing
a garland of flowers
that smelled of cordite.
He celebrated in the graveyard
where his good friends
lay shoulder to shoulder.
Such a patriot—flags and guns
and 'Victory!'—it's why
he never wanted to see another country,
some foreign country.
'That graveyard fence,' he said,
'is the only border I care to cross.'

*

He comes home from the market
carrying an empty bag
and I can't bear to look,
I stay out of his way. 'Victory!'
he yells. 'Did I fight for this—
for swindlers, for black marketeers?'
My mother pulls him into the kitchen
and pours a brandy. I stay
out of his way; I can't bear to think
of the photograph where he walks
into the town from the hills, garlanded,
carrying his Russian gun,
yelling, 'Victory! Victory! Victory!'

THE BRIDGE

One morning, a week or two before
the war started in earnest,
a film crew arrived in Ruža's village
bringing with them chaos and cold cash.

They built a second village in a day;
in less than half a day
they built a bridge, while local craftsmen
looked on, restless and shame-faced.

The villagers held out their hands:
in one they found dollars,
in the other buckskin and war-paint.

Their job was to fall from trees
shot through the heart, or fall
down a cliff-side, whacking
from rock to rock, shot through the heart,
or throw themselves off the bank and into the shallows,
shot clean through the heart.

Each night they would treat their bruises
with good Bosnian brandy and herbs.

*

One morning, a day or two before
the war started in earnest,
the villagers woke to find their second home
gone, the film crew gone, the money gone.
The only thing left was the bridge
which no one wanted to cross.

Now I watch Ruža as she writes a letter
to her brother, who lives
on the other side of the river. Even at night
you can see the corpses
floating downstream like shadows.

As she writes, bent to the page, she casts
a shadow in the shape of a bridge.
One hand is raised
to cover the scar on her neck left by an extra
who let go with his bow and arrow
before anyone had called 'Action'.

A COMMON STORY

Sarajevo, January 1993.
My friend put his wife and children on the bus
to God-knows-where,
and wrote on the frozen window, *I am with you.*

After that moment he wrote no more. I signed
his army ID card; I wrote
his requests for transfer to God-knows-where; I wrote
the first appeal, I wrote the second;
I wrote love-letters to his wife
and kissed his children each a hundred times.

I wanted to sign these letters: 'From someone whose words
have been sluiced into the sewer
by whoever cleans the shit and snow off buses.'

When they brought him to the hospital, it seemed
that half his body was missing.
I ran to read him a letter from his wife—
the first letter she'd sent—a love-letter
I'd written as fast as I could.
                          He didn't hear me.
He was breathless, dying for breath,
trying to find enough breath to say out loud
the words that had been sluiced into the sewer
by whoever cleans the shit and snow off buses.

LAMENT FOR VIJEĆNICA

The National Library burned for three days last August and the
city was choked with black snow.

Set free from the stack, characters wandered the streets, mingling
with passers-by and the souls of dead soldiers.

I saw Werther sitting on the ruined graveyard fence; I saw
Quasimodo swinging one-handed from a minaret.

Raskolnikov and Mersault whispered together for days in my
cellar; Gavroche paraded in camouflage fatigues;

Yossarian was already selling spares to the enemy; for a few
dinars young Sawyer would dive off Princip's bridge.

Each day—more ghosts and fewer people alive; and the terrible
suspicion formed that the shells fell just for me.

I locked myself in the house. I leafed through tourist guides. I
didn't come out until the radio told me

how they'd taken ten tons of clinker from the deepest cellar of
the burned-out National Library.

THE ARRIVAL OF THE WOLF

The sheep are smiling as they welcome the wolf.
They like to show their teeth. They like the smell of blood.
They wave the greasy tea-towels that serve as flags.

Wolf, don't be confused: you're not the first.
They've seen a flock of despots in this town
but none has left his mark.

This is a time of chaos and roses smell of skin.
This tram is your limo. This mansion's Command HQ.
It is dark down corridors and the marble has eyes.

Beautiful women follow you everywhere
for a tuft of fur, a shed claw, a dribble of drool.
They want them for potions. They want them for souvenirs.

Look in the mirror, wolf; your teeth are bright
as a general's chest, but the glass doesn't show
that you drop the peppery spoor of deer;

it leads you astray, it leads you down dark
corridors and through the herbarium,
past fallen roofs, under decaying stars.

Welcome, wolf. These sheep have scented blood.
They smile; they are smiling down on you
from the windows of the requisitioned hotel.

They want to know: Are you a wolf,
or could it be that you're nothing more than the shadow
of the wolf that's shadowing you?

Someone winds the clock. Someone will wake
in the moment you fall asleep. Someone will draw
the blinds on your view of the forest.

A draught will come at your door. A hand will stop
at your bed, the hand of the assassin.
Mice will eat your despatches.

After that—a page in a textbook, a pelt
pegged up on a gable end, the sheep
smiling, smiling, smiling as they welcome the wolf.

THE ROMANCE OF PARCELS

Before long, the city was one vast lock-up.
Those who stayed—I praised them.
Those who went over the wire while they had the chance—
I secretly missed them.

Food parcels came from my brother.
My only clear memory
from that time is the image of my mother
reflected in our lacquered kitchen table;
the way I recall it, she is holding a can-opener.

Food parcels came from friends:
mostly flour, I think, and letters that saddened me more
than dying Sarajevo. Getting down
to the bottom of each box, I found a place
as bleak as the border-crossing where they all went over
to the land of letters and parcels.

Then came this other box: a box of hunger.
My mother touched me as she might have touched a child,
then disappeared. And when I think back on it
she seems to vanish (I'm sure I remember this)
into the sink—washed-up and washed away.

Now I look at myself in the lacquered table.
Now I ask myself for perhaps the thousandth time:
Is it true that only the brave and good
stayed in Sarajevo? In Sarajevo
where some fool starts to whistle
and we dive for cover. In Sarajevo
where day after day my wife demands to know
why her husband won't clear the blocked-up kitchen sink.

LEJLA'S SECRET

Dr Lejla, of the Department for Corpse
Identification, went mad; it was
a few days before the turn of the year.

She came out of the mortuary
at a dead run, scattering
Official Documentation all down the street,
then locked herself into her apartment.

If she heard a voice on the stairwell, she answered
with screams. At night she played the piano,
tuneless, at random,
and howled, tuneless, at random.

So what had she seen that day at the mortuary?
Everyone in the neighbourhood
worried away at the question;
soon we could talk of nothing else.

A spare-parts corpse—tits and cock,
stubble and maidenhair,
all cobbled together by killers who liked a joke?
A child in an open womb?
The sudden face of her late husband?

No one knew. But each time the barrage began,
our cellar-shelter became a nightmare-workshop;
fear of the guns was nothing
compared to our fear of Lejla's imagination.

Her building emptied out: some died, some left,
but still she played, trying to stir the Devil.
No one watched when they came to fetch her
on the first day of the New Year.
She had opened her veins.

Refugees live in her apartment, now. They sleep
right through the night.
The rest of us listen, right through the night,
to the sound of Lejla's piano.

BEGINNING AFTER EVERYTHING

After I buried my mother
(under fire, I sprinted from the graveyard)

after the soldiers came with my brother
wrapped in a tarp
(I gave them back his gun)

after the fire in the eyes of my children
as they ran to the cellar
(the rats ran ahead of them)

after I wiped the old woman's face
with a dishtowel
(terrified to reveal a face I knew)

after the ravenous dog
feasting on blood
(just another corpse in snipers' alley)

after everything

I wanted to write poems like newspaper reports,
so heartless, so cold,
that I could forget them, forget them
in the same moment that someone might ask me,
'Why do you write poems like newspaper reports?'

THE MICE OF WAR

By the second summer of the war
a million mice lived in the town:
two million, ten . . .
                But at night,
rats came out of the sewers
to swarm on hills of garbage;
they tore-up cats, they mobbed children.

Each dusk, we locked our doors
and, as if they'd made a deal,
the rats stayed in the streets
while the mice came inside.
They romped in the flour, they made clothes
in the wardrobes dance. The more we killed
the more there were to kill.
                      We trapped our first
behind the piano. He was called 'the artist'
for his cunning. After him we killed
dozens, hundreds, but only the first had a name.

I am trying to remember the name
of Sarajevo's first victim: first
of all the black statistics . . .

I have fetched a box of obituary notices
down from the attic. Inside are scraps of paper,
just scraps, and the wide eyes of the mice.

THE STORY OF BEŠO

After a year in the Aussie cane-fields
Bešo had had enough: enough
of the smoke gun, enough
of the thick, black scribble
of snakes the smoke smoked-out, enough
of the cane-cutters who sold him
their daughters for shirt-buttons.

On the day he left, the manager
explained a thing or two: 'They thought
you had special powers. Do you remember
laying aside the serum and the syringe?
That was the day they took you
for their mulla-mullung, you see?
Their figure-flinger, their ju-ju man,
their little tin god. Know why?
Only such a man could cock a snook
at those five seconds of live-or-die
after the bite.' Bešo turned away
to hide the sudden panic in his eyes.

He moved on, taking up
as a poacher in the Northern Territory.
A Czech marksman would nail
the crocs, and they'd float downstream
where Bešo waited
to gaff them and haul them aboard.
Business was good until the police arrived.
That was the day Bešo found out
his pistol lacked a firing pin . . .
When they were free and clear, the Czech
explained a thing or two: 'My shots
were risks we *had* to take—
different with you; but, anyway, what kind

of chance d'you think a man would have
with a wounded crocodile?' Bešo lit up
a cigarette, shaking the match
to kill it, wanting to give
his shaking hands something to do.

Where next? Sarajevo—where else?
Back home... But it took a shell clear through
his apartment, front to back,
before Bešo decided to join
our colony in the cellar. 'Move it, Bešo!'
I yelled as I ran downstairs. He grinned
as if I'd cracked a joke,
grinned and stepped into the blood
of a neighbour whose body we'd shifted
only a moment before. I thought: Perhaps
he didn't notice the blood. Perhaps
he's got the idea it's just today—
just today, the shelling, just today
the stiff on the stairs. Perhaps
someone should explain a thing or two,
someone should tell him the war
has lasted a year. A whole year.
Has already lasted a year.

THE CALENDAR

I heard the fall of a leaf from a calendar.
It was the leaf for the month of March.
The calendar belongs to a girl I know.

She spends each day checking the calendar
and watching her belly grow.
Whatever is in her womb
was nailed there by drunken soldiers in some camp.
It is something that feeds
on terrible images and a terrible silence.

What fills the images?
Her bloodstained dress, perhaps,
fluttering from a pole like a flag?

What breaks the silence?
The fall of the month of March?
The footstep of her tormentor—his face
the child's face, the face she will see
every day, every month, every year
for the rest of her life?

I don't know. I don't know.
All I heard was the fall of a leaf from a calendar.

LOVE STORY

Last spring, the story of Boško & Admira
was a Major Media Event.
They planned to leave Sarajevo
by crossing a bridge between the present
and the future. In truth,
what lay on the other side was the past.
Boško & Admira were dead
before they reached the middle of the bridge.

Headlines appeared in the international press:
Boško & Admira—a Bosnian Romeo & Juliet!
Boško & Admira—the love that knew no frontiers!
Boško & Admira—symbols of a nation divided!
Boško & Admira—the futility of war!
Every paper carried a shot of the dead lovers.

My friend, Prsić, is a soldier; he guards the bridge.
Throughout those early spring days,
he watched the bodies of Boško & Admira
swelling and rotting, swarmed on by maggots,
by flies, by carrion crows.

He would curse and strap on a gas-mask
whenever the light spring breeze
blew in his direction.

IN ROUND THE BACK

I've got one eye on the front door
when they come in round the back—
certain officers
with gold buttons for eyes.
They are searching for my gold-
rimmed spectacles;
they are searching for a novel point of view.

Their gloves leave prints—chevrons
or bars, according to rank—
on the plates that bear my reflection,
on the glasses I never drink from,
on the windows convex with confinement.

Then they leave, telling jokes
about women I used to love.

*

It's becoming a habit: the police, now,
in through the back,
each with a rubber pencil tucked into his belt.
They eavesdrop on my books; the books
snuffle and whine
like dogs left out in the snow.

Then they leave (the way they came, of course)
and their fingers remain on the doorknob,
but their uniforms bob and fade
like cans in the river.

*

Tell me this: why do postmen
come in round the back, and why
are they carrying bags
that reek of formalin, and why
are they kitted-out with army-issue boots?

They form ranks and march through the bathroom.
They are searching
for my pyjamas, which I've tucked away
in a box of carbon paper. I ask them,
'What do you want
with my pyjamas?' and just for a moment
there is something in their eyes
that tells me everything,
something tender like April.

Then they leave and slam the door
and the room flares up in darkness.

*

I've got one eye on the front door,
where the shadow of someone's hand
covers the doorbell.

Enter someone.
Someone should enter.

RUŽA AND THE TRAMS

All that remains of Ruža
is the weasel-fur from the collar of her coat
and a monthly pass for the tram.

Now all the trams
rust on the rails, and Ruža
takes long walks with the angels.

Her wardrobe is hung with shadows.
The only thing real is the greasy fingerprint
left on her tram-pass by the conductor.

I wonder if he's still alive.
I wonder whether, in some other life, his fingers
might touch the weasel-fur on Ruža's collar.

I don't know. Honest to God, I don't
know how to think about that
after a year of war.

A DREAM

Asleep—dreaming
that you are asleep and dreaming
of something easy to forget . . .

You'll wake and pick from your mouth
whatever's left
of a broken mirror; you'll find

a pair of crutches
in the crawlspace beneath your bed; the day
will limp outside as if it were a day

like any other; and perhaps you'll notice, but later,
a little later, your portrait
on the pillow, sketched in blood.

THE NEXT STEP

It took three years of war
to send my neighbour mad. Three years
in the slaughterhouse we call 'our town'.
He had good reason.

From the top of a tall poplar
just opposite the Presidency building
he swayed and cursed the state,
the government, the army,
the police and God;
then he turned on us, all stock-
still, all staring up: 'So what
are you looking at? You'll do
the same tomorrow.'

Oh, and he got that right!
That was the worst fear by far,
that was the maggot under the skin . . .

One day you find yourself
at the top, the tip, the birdless
brow of a tree, and you don't know how
you got there, and you don't
give a shit for the fools
turning up to watch, and you don't give a shit
for the government officers
who are shaking the tree while you curse
the state, the government, the army, the police,
and not forgetting God. You look across
at the Presidency building, its pillars
and posts, its flounces
and furbelows and you think, *The tree
is older than the building, yes, the tree*

is older, yes, the tree
has been here longer, much longer, the tree
is sure to outlast the place, the tree
the tree the tree the tree
is the safest place to be.

CURTAINS

I wake you in the middle of the night. I say,
'I'm having a crazy dream. Come and dream it with me.'
You smile and turn over.

I wanted to let you know
that our bed has become a nation-state, the sheet
its flag, and just over there,
by the border-crossing, a Lapp
and an Aboriginal are leafing through
a book on American Indians.
I wanted to ask, 'What do you make of that?'

I wanted to say I'd noticed
that our blanket is cut from the self-same cloth
we use for the blackout.
And I wanted to tell you how, for years,
the way you smile in your sleep
had kept me from sleeping.

CONSEQUENCES

A fly on the TV screen dots the President's eye
as he warns of the terrible days to come.
Behind the President is a flag unfurled.

Beyond that flag, a woman is counting cash
from the sale of the morning paper.
Her son is sleeping, tucked up
on the cobbles, his hands black with newsprint.
Tacked up on the kiosk,
a cutting from the paper shows the son
with the President, giving and getting
a firm handshake. It's easy to see
how ashamed the poor boy is of his dirty hands.

Beyond the woman and the kiosk,
the Faculty's star pupil,
now a truck-driver, unwraps a sandwich
from yesterday's front page
while a JCB loads earth into his dumpster.

He's recalling how many anthems
were sung for this earth, how many tears
shed on this earth, how many young men
lie in this good earth; or else he's counting
the bullet holes in the cab of his truck; or else
he's thinking that sandwiches
get smaller every day.

A wind stirs the flag. The boy stirs.
The early-morning edition
flaps at the smashed side-windows of the truck,
then clatters off unread. It carries
a portrait of the President
and a warning of the terrible days ahead.

THE OLD ONES

The old ones of Sarajevo are disappearing,
slow but sure,
without formality, without farewells.

They stop for a rest between here and there
and simply fade. They stoop
for a clothes peg and become the earth.

Next day they turn up in the morning paper,
modest in black, standing neatly in line,
then they shuffle off to give space to the war.

In their rooms you might find a diary, or some letters;
a new suit bought for the funeral
and laid down years ago.

A breeze frets the curtains: is that the old ones
taking a last look,
or whispering their names to us in case we forget?

*

Remember that retired captain from the ground floor back?
It took us half a day to bury him.
The snipers were on-song and, in the end,

his grave became our slit-trench,
wet and wormy, the sappy smell of severed roots,
while the crossfire hummed above our heads.

For three years he kept in touch
with an imaginary son: one thousand
and ninety-five letters, filed in shoe boxes.

Remember that former employee
of the former bank? Refugee kids were making paper darts
from pages of his diary. I offered

a square of chocolate each, they held out for the bar
and were half-way home before I realised
each entry was carefully penned in invisible ink.

Remember that old guy whose family
had been butchered before his eyes? Remember
the battery-radio he carried everywhere?

He gave me that a couple of days before
we carried him out of the cellar.
It had no batteries, and the on/off switch was buggered.

*

My little collection of memorabilia. . .
if it ever had any meaning, the meaning's gone
along with the old ones,

unless there's something in this:
I didn't think to check the news from the front
today, yesterday, or even the day before,

being so completely caught up
in the silent airwaves, the empty
diary, the letters to no one.

HAVING A WORD WITH GOD

It started out as a quarrel,
like a married couple
with a case of adultery pending,
still in love
but hot for divorce.

Then he took up the role
of the calm, cool one
—distant look, half smile—
while I blattered on
with back-to-back questions
all of them sounding like answers.

'You can see everything,
can you see that impetigo-
pink circle,
third finger, left hand
of the old woman
who sold the very last thing
she had in the world?
Can you see that single
shoe on the garbage dump?
Can you see the boy in calipers
who begs at the church door, trying
to raise the black-market price
of his grandmother's ring?
Have I mentioned
I wouldn't believe in you
if you knocked me aside the head?'

I woke up to an ashtray
full of butts,
and didn't begin to feel
even half-way good
until the hangover hit.

When I finally raised a laugh
it sounded for all the world
like the laugh of a man
who's just agreed
a 'full-and-final'
with his Jezebel of a wife.

He puts his boot
to the elevator, then walks
down from the thousandth floor,
impatient for a glimpse
of the fool walking up.
The fool on the up and up.

CHRISTMAS

'I'm blind,' I say. I don't speak again
for a very long time. Of course,
I'm lying about being blind: if I look
out of the window, to where
the children are singing carols, I see
how the snow seems to fetch a rainbow;
I see frozen songbirds fall
from the branches; I see a butcher haul
a slaughtered lamb down the street.

It is night. An icon burns in the stove.
There's a seamless drone from the airport
that makes me want to weep.
'I am blind,' I say, 'I am blind.'
She doesn't say a word. She beats
the Devil's tattoo on the tabletop.

'I've forgotten,' I whisper. I don't speak again
for a very long time. Of course,
I'm lying about having forgotten: I think back
to hoofprints in the snow and dogs on a leash.
It was a manhunt. I remember my father laughed
when I barked at the birds.

'Have you ever noticed how a vacuum-cleaner sounds
like a plane in take-off, or how
a TV left on too long will fix a room
with a hot and heavy smell? Have you noticed
the depth of frost?' I ask her.
'Have you noticed this incredible frost at all?'
She's got nothing to say for herself.
She might not have heard.

I won't speak again. I'll sit here and watch
the traffic lights adapting endlessly
to whatever's best. That's me, I'm just like that.
A whole universe buzzes above
the control tower: isn't that strange?
Fish in the depths are strange—the way they live.
The smell of hay in an orchard
is too strange for words. Now and then,
someone winks from the bottle:
the genie, the Puck of plum brandy.
'Can you see me?' I ask. 'Can you see any jot
of me, any tittle?' She nods, but of course
she's lying. As if I cared, as if
she could understand the half of what I say.

A SHORT LECTURE ON LIFE

He comes in to the room at a run,
my father, weeping,
a newspaper in his fist
with my name shining out
at the top of the obit. column
along with a recent photograph:
muzzy, but me.

'How could you do it?' he asks.
'Why didn't you warn me?
My pension's a pittance;
how will I pay for the box,
the bearers, the wake?'

'That's not me,' I tell him;
'you think that's me? Of course not.
See my hand turning
this page in my notebook? Hear
the pencil whispering
as I write my name?
This is me; here I am; still alive.'

He gives a sour laugh.
'What does that prove?
A paper to say you're alive,
a paper to say you're dead—
same difference, except
one's the impartial view.'

'I'm talking to you,' I say,
'can't you hear me? Listen:
this is my voice saying "Can't
you hear me?" What more do you need?'

He replies, 'Forget it, forget all that
Can't-you-hear-me stuff.
When I read the report
of your death, the first thing
I heard was your voice,
as any father would.
I heard it just the way
I'm hearing it now; and you said
just what you're saying now.'

He won't stand still for any more.
He's off downstairs at a lick
wiping his tears on his cuff.
'Look,' I call after him, 'listen,
I know damn well I'm alive,
there's proof, hard proof,
there's official documentation,
with stamps and ribbons and seals,
that says "Born—" and the date
and place and other facts, including
"father's name". What's just another
misprint compared to that?'

'Don't yell at me,' he yells.
'What the hell do you know
about life and death? What do you know
about official documentation?
Don't tell me about facts—
I know all about *facts!*'

He waits for me to speak,
I wait for him—a good
two minutes, then I hear
the floorboards creak
as he makes for the street.

I'm not dead—here's my notebook
and pencil; the official
documentation; this poem.

Why does he give me such grief?

WHAT'S LEFT?

What's left of our rebellion?
It wasn't mentioned in this morning's papers.

What's left of our manifesto?
Only a few remember: the brave and the craven.

What's left of our posters and banners?
A smell of ink; a smell of shame
as we pass in ragged procession
walking our dogs, taking our kids for a walk.

The flags have lost their colour,
but the street is the same, there's that same
cloud of sparrows we put to flight
as we rushed to the meeting-place
glowing with new ideas, new life, new hope.

What's left of the candles that burned so fast
there was never time to count the conspirators?

The only light is the rose of cigarettes
as we take one final, nervous drag
then wet our fingers to pinch away the coal
making comet-trails fly up in darkness.

The only sound is our voices, like damp squibs;
the *sotto voce* of lies in history primers.

Each New Year's Day in Bosnia
starts with a cake and ends with dirty plates.
Except for this simple metaphor
I could tell myself that nothing happened:
no banners, no flags, no street, no meeting-place.
Except for the sparrows as witness
I would disappear entirely.

Under my window, under this empty room,
this empty space, a boy
throws a firecracker into the snow,
putting the sparrows to flight.

SARAJEVO SPRING

It is spring again. The spring is coming.
It is coming in
on crutches. Swallows nest in the ruins.

Someone has strung a clothes-line
in the graveyard
and a hundred diapers semaphore the wind.

Peace surprised us: we needed more time
to pretend we deserved it, more time
to be 'the survivors',

as if we had plans, as if we knew
what next, as if
our dreams were not all of seagulls and the sea.

Peace is like a virus, a light fever.
Peace makes our Sunday suits
restless; it makes our shoes shuffle.

Soldiers wander the streets legless on slivovitz
asking, 'What next? What next?'
They won't go home

to collect their demob papers, they won't
hand in their uniforms;
well, what did you expect?

They needed more time, more time
like the boy we carried feet first from the movie-house,
wiped out by a happy ending;

like our neighbours, who've clean forgotten
how to keep a good row going;
like our local hero, a four-hundred-metre man,

who sits all day by the running track
in his wheelchair
as if it might suddenly come to him: what next.

Soon it will be medals and flags, a coat of whitewash
for the orphanage walls. The children carry
family albums with them

wherever they go. My friend carries
a child's winter glove. I think
he needs more time for this, more time, I think

peace has made us less than ourselves, and spring
is coming, hobble-
clop, hobble-clop, hobble-clop.

AFTERWORD

We are still alive. I would like to thank Amela Simić, Susan Sontag, Phil Robinson, David Harsent, Christopher Merrill, Kris Janowski, Nigel Osborne, Vesa Toijonen, Paolo Dilonardo, Rada Gavrilović, Boris A. Novak, Sandro Lunin, Marcy Gerstein and Ferida Duraković, without whose friendship my life would more resemble this book.

G.S.

OXFORD POETS

Fleur Adcock

Moniza Alvi

Jospeh Brodsky

Basil Bunting

Tessa Rose Chester

Daniela Crăsnaru

Michael Donaghy

Keith Douglas

D. J. Enright

Roy Fisher

Ida Affleck Graves

Ivor Gurney

David Harsent

Gwen Harwood

Anthony Hecht

Zbigniew Herbert

Tobias Hill

Thomas Kinsella

Brad Leithauser

Derek Mahon

Jamie McKendrick

Sean O'Brien

Alice Oswald

Peter Porter

Craig Raine

Zsuzsa Rakovszky

Henry Reed

Christopher Reid

Stephen Romer

Carole Satyamurti

Peter Scupham

Jo Shapcott

Penelope Shuttle

Goran Simić

Anne Stevenson

George Szirtes

Grete Tartler

Edward Thomas

Charles Tomlinson

Marina Tsvetaeva

Chris Wallace-Crabbe

Hugo Williams